The Little Black Book Of Fun Dates!

Exciting & Fun Date Night Ideas!

The Little Black Book of Fun Dates

Copyright © 2015 by Page Cole

TABLE OF CONTENTS

GUYS IN CHARGE 8

NINE RULES FOR DATE NIGHT 9

PAJAMA NIGHT OUT 10

A NIGHT AT THE MUSEUM 11

STRIKE OR SPARE 13

FAST FOOD IN THE PARK 14

DOLLAR MOVIE ROULETTE 16

GIDDY UP 17

BOOK'EM DANNO 19

LIFE'S A BEACH 20

ROLLERCOASTERS & FUNNEL CAKES 22

DON'T BE CRABBY... OR DO 23

PUTT THAT PUTT 25

THE GREAT WHITE WAY 26

X MARKS THE SPOT 28

BEARING GIFTS 29

WATERFRONT STROLL 31

WELL THAT'S UNUSUAL 32

TAKE ME OUT TO THE BALLGAME 34

LASER TAG, YOU'RE IT 35

GO SPEED RACER 37

PUTTING DOWN ROOTS 38

DRIVE-IN DATE 40

WEDDING CRASHERS 41

PAPARAZZI & SELFIES 43

OOOO LA LA 44

HE'S A FRIENDLY, GIANT MOUSE 46

LOCAL FLAVOR OF EVENTS 47

ROLLER DERBY QUEEN 49

SAY "I DO" ALL OVER AGAIN 50

ROMANTIC NIGHT OUT 52

DATE ALA MODE 53

I LOVE U FOREVER 55

CRUISING WITH THE TOP DOWN 56

GET AWAY GO AWAY 58

STRIKE A POSE 59

AQUA-MASSAGE ME 61

HOME SPA TREATMENT 62

BIRTHDAY MUSIC TIME 64

CHICK FLICK MOVIE TIME 65

LEAVIN' ON A JET PLANE 67

TAKE IT FOR A TEST DRIVE 68

THRIFTY NIGHT OUT 70

PRIME CUT 71

PUT IT IN REVERSE 73

WORKIN' AT THE CAR WASH 74

HOOP IT UP 76

JAZZ IT UP 77

FANCY SCHMANCY 79

PICNIC IN THE PARK 80

A SHOT IN THE DARK 82

BACK TO NATURE 83

GIRL'S IN CHARGE **84**

Nine Rules For the Night...85

    SHIRTS & TACOS.. 86

    GOODWILL EACH OTHER....................................... 88

    BOWLING FOR YOUR BABY 89

    PICNIC IN THE GARDEN 91

    MAKE OUT MOVIE.. 92

    RIB TICKLER COWBOY 94

    PICK A PIC & BOOK A BOOK 95

    A SHADY KIND OF DATE 97

    SMELLS LIKE TEEN SPIRIT.................................... 98

    FLIRT THE NIGHT AWAY 100

    DEDICATED TO THE ONE YOU LOVE........................ 101

    THE SUN WILL COME OUT TOMORROW 103

    MALL EXPEDITION 104

    TEDDY CONSTRUCTION 106

    ON THE WATERFRONT.. 107

    SOUNDTRACK OF YOUR LIFE 109

    MY MOST FAVORITE THING 110

    LET'S MONKEY AROUND..................................... 112

    FUN A LA MODE 113

    PUTTING DOWN SOME ROOTS............................... 115

    GLORY DAYS.. 116

    I STILL DO.. 118

    MY KIND OF COUPONS 119

    SLEEPWEAR OR NOT TO WEAR 121

    I DON'T WANNA GROW UP 122

ICE, ICE BABY 124

SKATING INTO THE GOLDEN YEARS 125

VOW TO VOW AGAIN 127

SCRAPPING OVER DINNER.. 128

AMATEUR VANDALS 130

GIDDY UP 131

DRIVING ME CRAZY 133

B & B FOR YOU AND HE 134

LIVE SHOTS, DEAD SHOTS.. 136

SECRET MASSAGE.. 138

PAMPER YOUR MAN 139

SING, SING A SONG.. 140

A NIGHT ON THE TOWN 142

FLY AWAY 143

KING OF THE ROAD.. 145

THRIFTINESS IS NEXT GOODWILL.. 146

DINNER ON THE LAKE... 148

REVERSE DATE 150

SHOE POLISH SHOWS YOU CARE 151

BATTER, BATTER, BATTER SWING.. 152

TASTE THE RAINBOW 154

CALLING DR. LOVE 155

PICNIC PLAYGROUND 157

YOU CRAZY ANIMAL 158

NATURE CALLS 160

GUYS IN CHARGE

NINE RULES FOR DATE NIGHT

(and every night for that matter!)

1) Open every door for her!!!

2) Listen a lot, and remember she's the most important person in your life!!!

3) Do everything you can to make this a night she'll cherish!!!

4) Try to stick to the guidelines for your date as close as you can; unless you can do better!!!

5) Shave & shower before the date!!!

6) Wear something nice, and try to look sharp for her– it's a date!

7) If you need childcare for your kids, then you arrange for it, and confirm it on that date!!!

8) If you run into someone you know while on the date, politely GET AWAY QUICKLY!!!

9) Touch, talk, smile, laugh, kiss, hug... a bunch!!!

Pajama Night Out

Pre Date Prep

Buy dozen flowers- eleven of one kind, one of another; attach a note that says "In every bunch there's one who stands out– and you're that one.

The Big Date

Go to the mall, and shop for and buy a fun pair of pajamas for each other... then head to a Mexican restaurant, and take turns sharing food.

During the Date

Spend some time in silence, gazing into each other's eyes; then spend some time talking about places you each want to visit on vacation- make plans if you want!

Closing the Night Out

Draw her a bubble bath– and when she is ready to get out, give her a large towel that has been warmed in the dryer.

A Night at the Museum

Pre Date Prep

Write a "Thank You" note to her parents for all she has meant to you. Also, for this event, both of you take the opportunity to dress nice- coat & tie for you, and a dress for her!

The Big Date

Visit an art museum; after the museum, go a fancy restaurant for dinner.

During the Date

Make a list of 5 things you like about your spouse, and share those with each other. After you both share, give her a copy of the letter you have already written and sent to her parents thanking them for the job they did with her.

Closing the Night Out

Sit in the car in the driveway and cuddle for 15 minutes. You can kiss, count stars, listen to music- just don't talk about what needs done to the flower beds!

STRIKE OR SPARE

Pre Date Prep

Have a giant banner printed at an office supply business. Say something wonderful and romantic, and put it up in front of the bowling alley.

The Big Date

Take her bowling; then hit your favorite pizza or Chinese food joint.

During the Date

Take turns sharing your most favorite memories of time with each other.

Closing the Night Out

Change the sheets on your bed at home, as well as the pillow covers. If it's been a while since you've had new sheets, then go buy a set of high quality sheets and pillow covers for the bed, and put those on the bed.

FAST FOOD IN THE PARK

Pre Date Prep

Buy her one daisy, with the note attached– "She loves me, she loves me not"; make sure there are an odd number of petals on the daisy.

The Big Date

Rush home, change into the nicest clothes you can in 10 minutes, stop by a fast food restaurant, and have a picnic lunch at a local park or scenic recreation area.

During the Date

Over dinner, talk about what your desired things to own, desired people to meet or desired experiences to have.

Closing the Night Out

Write "I Love You" on the bathroom mirror with soap after she goes to sleep.

DOLLAR MOVIE ROULETTE

Pre Date Prep

Ask your wife's best friend to help you buy a present that she's certain your wife would like- give her a budget.

The Big Date

Write the names of the movies showing at the dollar movie on separate pieces of paper. Randomly pick one, and then go to that movie, then take her to a unique pub or themed restaurant for a fun dinner.

During the Date

Kiss a lot during the movie; take turns initiating the kiss.

Closing the Night Out

Bring her chocolate covered strawberries, or strawberries and powdered sugar, as you get ready for bed.

GIDDY UP

Pre Date Prep

Buy a nice inexpensive necklace, and drape it around a teddy bears neck.

The Big Date

Go horseback riding; then head out for dinner to a BBQ joint you've never tried before.

During the Date

Talk about the most fun you've ever had with your clothes on with each other; and the most fun you've had with your clothes off with each other.

Closing the Night Out

Have a bouquet of "I Love You" balloons waiting for her when you get back.

BOOK'EM DANNO

Pre Date Prep

Buy a small bottle of her favorite perfume (get advice from one of her close friends if you don't know), and give it to her.

The Big Date

Visit a local bookstore, and with a $15 limit, find the funniest, wackiest book that you think your spouse would like; then look at your books over dinner at a sandwich shop.

During the Date

Take your wedding pictures with you, and spend time looking back through your pictures.

Closing the Night Out

Stop and order one banana split, two spoons. Take turns feeding each other ice cream.

LIFE'S A BEACH

Pre Date Prep

Buy a pair of earrings (get advice from one of her close friends if you don't know) and put them on a teddy bear; also, get a basket, and preorder you're a picnic lunch of sandwiches, chips, cookies & drinks from a local restaurant- pick them up right before the date.

The Big Date

Drive to a nearby lake, and spend time walking barefoot along the shoreline, or dangling them off of a dock.

During the Date

Each one spend 10 minutes writing a love note to your spouse. Be sure that you bring the blank note cards and pens.

Closing the Night Out

Go to a drive-in restaurant, and order one large drink, and two straws.

Rollercoasters & Funnel Cakes

Pre Date Prep

Purchase her favorite scent of candle and give it to her.

The Big Date

Go to an amusement park, ride the rides, and try not to throw up; eat dinner at the park, or swing over to a nearby restaurant that you've never tried. Order an appetizer you've never tried and enjoy!

During the Date

Talk about the "firsts" in your life; first time you met, first date, first kiss, first Christmas, first time you said I love you, etc.

Closing the Night Out

Stop at a coffee shop like Java Dave's or Starbucks and enjoy some overpriced coffee.

Don't Be Crabby... or Do

Pre Date Prep

Purchase a fun, cute watch, and have it inscribed on the back with something like "I always have time for you".

The Big Date

Go shopping, and buy matching ball caps, shirts, SOMETHING... after shopping, then go to a local seafood restaurant for a fun dinner... and be sure and tell them it's her birthday... You might want to buy matching shirts there to remind you of the date.

During the Date

Flirt with each other during the date.

Closing the Night Out

Have a package of her favorite ice cream waiting at home, and make her a bowl with all her favorite toppings.

PUTT THAT PUTT

Pre Date Prep

Buy a romantic mushy card, and actually write your own note on it too– something longer than "Love, (your name).

The Big Date

Play miniature golf; then take her to a romantic Italian restaurant.

During the Date

Call several radio stations and ask them to play and dedicate your favorite songs to each other.

Closing the Night Out

Carry her over the threshold of your house when you return home, and tell her, "I would marry you and live this life all over again."

THE GREAT WHITE WAY

Pre Date Prep

Buy her a CD from her favorite artist, or one that she has been wanting, and give it to her.

The Big Date

Take her to a musical or Broadway production at a local theater or performing art center. Before the production, take her somewhere that offers patio or rooftop seating, and make reservations to insure you get a prime seat.

During the Date

Hold hands during the program, and look into each other's eyes during the romantic songs.

Closing the Night Out

Split a large fries and coke at McDonalds- talk about what your dreams are for 10 & 20 years from now.

X Marks the Spot

Pre Date Prep

Count the number of days that you have been together, and have a cookie decorated at the mall and waiting, saying "Happy (# of) days!".

The Big Date

Go on a Mall Treasure Hunt at a local mall; take $10 each, and 30 minutes, and buy as many fun or cute trinkets for each other.

During the Date

Meet back at the food court in the mall, and feed each other whatever food you order; talk about the most unique people you've ever met, the most unusual presents you've ever received, the most peculiar place you've ever been– all of the weird things.

Closing the Night Out

Spend 10 minutes of time brainstorming for your next date; find a date on the calendar and book it.

BEARING GIFTS

Pre Date Prep

Dig out a picture of your wife's wedding bouquet; take it to a florist, and have it recreated, and give it to her.

The Big Date

Take her to the "Build a Teddy Bear" Store, and let her build her own personalized teddy bear; then go to a "build your own burrito/sandwich/etc." restaurant, and have them build your dinner!

During the Date

Kiss at every stoplight, or every time you pass a red car.

Closing the Night Out

Finish the evening with a piece of pie somewhere, and talk about your favorite things and funniest memories about weddings- yours and others!

WATERFRONT STROLL

Pre Date Prep

Buy her an inexpensive music box with one of her favorite songs playing.

The Big Date

Walk along a local river walkway, and take a basket with food & drinks to snack on; sandwiches or chicken drumsticks are perfect for a picnic... spaghetti is not.

During the Date

Watch the sunset together, and kiss as the sun is setting.

Closing the Night Out

Talk about what makes you really– really happy, sad, scared, excited, angry, aroused.

Well That's Unusual

Pre Date Prep

Buy her one of as many different colors of carnations that you can find.

The Big Date

Visit a unique museum- a sports museum, musical museum, gun museum- and follow it up with dinner @ her favorite kind of restaurant- so you will have to know her favorite kind of food, or ask her.

During the Date

Sit and talk about what you think are the most attractive traits of your spouse, both internal & external.

Closing the Night Out

If the weather is good, sit under the stars someplace private and snuggle; if not, go to IHOP or other late night hangout and do the same thing.

TAKE ME OUT TO THE BALLGAME

Pre Date Prep

Take out an ad in the local newspaper, declaring your love for your spouse, and give a copy of it to her on the date; or make a sign and post it at a prominent exit off of the highway.

The Big Date

Attend a sporting event; eat hot dogs at the game, or when it's through, head to a fast food joint for a late night dinner... but make it a little fancy– bring along a cloth tablecloth, and a candle to make it romantic.

During the Date

Buy trinkets- pennants, caps, etc. for each other.

Closing the Night Out

Make a list of your sizes, favorite colors, favorite scents, aftershave/perfume, food, store to shop in, restaurant, and any other favorites- swap lists and surprise each other with the next week.

Laser Tag, You're It

Pre Date Prep

Buy her a stuffed monkey, and attach the note "Let's monkey around".

The Big Date

Play laser tag together; after laser tag is over, eat dinner with a buffet with lots of food choices.

During the Date

Work as a team to gang up and take out everyone else, starting with the small, weak and helpless people playing.

Closing the Night Out

Go get a snow cone, and talk about what your favorites are- movies, music, song, actor/actress, or any other favorites.

GO SPEED RACER

Pre Date Prep

Buy 1 or 2 one-time use cameras, as well as buying or finding matching shirts to wear on your date.

The Big Date

Go to a family fun center and ride the go-carts, play the games, act goofy; after some fun play time, head out to restaurant with a reputation for great food and awesome desserts. Plan on having both!

During the Date

Have as many different people as you can find to take pictures of the two of you.

Closing the Night Out

Don't forget to order dessert… but order and eat dessert first! Each order something different, and switch when you've eaten half of yours. Let her know you're eating dessert because the best shouldn't have to wait for last… and that because that's true, you want to recommit to making her the first priority in your life.

Putting Down Roots

Pre Date Prep

Buy a matching pair of goofy shirts for the two of you, and wear them on the date.

The Big Date

Go to a nursery, home improvement store or someplace similar and spend time shopping for special plants, bushes or trees; buy one that you can call "your" tree or bush, and plant it together the next day.

During the Date

Talk about what the most important things are to each of you for building a strong relationship, a strong family, a strong faith.

Closing the Night Out

Go to a burger place, and order a different burger than you've ever tried... and then take turns feeding each other your burger and fries.

DRIVE-IN DATE

Pre Date Prep

Put together a small ice chest complete with her favorite pop, candies and snacks.

The Big Date

Go to the drive in movie... if it's a good movie, watch the movie a little; if it's not, then find something else to do... since the movie starts late, you'll want to eat dinner before the movie... try a family owned pizza joint or greasy spoon café.

During the Date

Take some breaks from the car and walk around the drive in. Talk about your favorite experiences in high school.

Closing the Night Out

Before bed, offer to give her a back rub or foot rub.

WEDDING CRASHERS

Pre Date Prep

Check in the paper for a wedding taking place at one of the large churches in your area, and find directions; also, buy an inexpensive costume bracelet for her.

The Big Date

Rush home, dress up nice, and invite yourself to complete strangers wedding... stay for cake and punch; after the wedding & reception, take her to eat at an out of the way restaurant with atmosphere; be sure to call for reservations.

During the Date

Write love notes back and forth to each other during the ceremony.

Closing the Night Out

Come up with as many fun ways to celebrate your next five or ten wedding anniversaries. Brainstorm a list of places you could go, things you could do, how long you would stay, etc.

Paparazzi & Selfies

Pre Date Prep

Buy her an inexpensive gold locket, and cut out a picture of yourself to fit inside... Give it to her by asking her to close her eyes, and then put it on her.

The Big Date

Take a Polaroid camera (instant pictures) and have strangers take pictures of you both (waving, kissing, acting silly, striking a pose) at a local boardwalk or riverfront, at the mall, the grocery store, WHEREVER & WHATEVER! End up for dinner at a restaurant with a nice view of the city or other picturesque setting.

During the Date

Over your favorite soda, each of you finish the following statements- Love is, Sadness is, Happiness is, Anger is, Peace is, Disappointment is, etc.

Closing the Night Out

Take a walk in the moonlight... hold hands and stop & kiss every block or every five minutes.

Oooo La La

Pre Date Prep

Buy her a gift certificate to Victoria's Secret.

The Big Date

Go to Victoria's Secret together, and pick out something with her gift certificate together... Then go to a department store or Wal-Mart– somewhere, ANYWHERE but Victoria's Secret, and pick out some night wear for you!

During the Date

Over dinner at her favorite kind of restaurant (Mexican, Chinese, whatever), answer the following question... "If you could have five wishes, what would they be, and why?" Take turns sharing your wishes.

Closing the Night Out

Go home for a while, if there are no kids there, and try on your new sleepwear... If they are home, then find a coffee bar or frozen custard stand to enjoy some time together.

HE'S A FRIENDLY, GIANT MOUSE

Pre Date Prep

Buy her a trophy, and have a name plate put on it calling her "The World's Best Friend".

The Big Date

Go to Chuck E Cheese's, and play games and eat pizza– act like a kid and have some fun.

During the Date

Over dinner, answer the following questions- 'What do you want to be remembered for?"; "If you had only had one day to live, what would you do during that day?"; "What things can I do today & tomorrow to make you feel special?"

Closing the Night Out

Stop for dessert your favorite ice cream place- one Sundae or Banana Split, two spoons.

LOCAL FLAVOR OF EVENTS

Pre Date Prep

Ask one of her friends what her favorite "scent" is, and buy her some potpourri in that scent.

The Big Date

Browse online, or check out the local paper ahead of time for a special local event.

During the Date

Go to dinner at nice restaurant with a broad selection of food, and over dinner talk about what you think the perfect house would be like... the perfect job... the perfect vacation.

Closing the Night Out

Go to a drive-in restaurant and have slushies for dessert... or hot chocolate!

ROLLER DERBY QUEEN

Pre Date Prep

Ask one of her friends what her favorite "scent" is, and buy her a decorative candle in that scent; use it in the basket you prepare with a cloth tablecloth, nice silverware, crystal glasses & cloth napkins.

The Big Date

Take her roller skating… Take her to her favorite fast food restaurant or to a 50's themed restaurant if there is one nearby, but set the table nice with tablecloth, napkins, candle, crystal and silverware.

During the Date

Talk about what you want to do when you retire.

Closing the Night Out

Stop for an ice cream cone or frozen custard after dinner.

Say "I Do" All Over Again

Pre Date Prep

If possible, contact the minister who married you, and arrange to have him meet you somewhere romantic to perform a renewal of your vows.

The Big Date

Meet the minister at a prearranged location, and have him do a repeat or a renewal of your wedding vows.

During the Date

Take your wedding pictures with you, and following the wedding, and over a romantic dinner at a fancy Italian restaurant, and once you're seated and have ordered, pull out the pictures.

Closing the Night Out

Talk about what your favorite memories of your wedding day were; funny, serious, sexy– all of them! Before you go to bed that night, tell her WHY if you had it to do all over again, you WOULD marry her all over again.

ROMANTIC NIGHT OUT

Pre Date Prep

Make a list of the most important people in her life-
parents, best friend, kids, boss, teachers, neighbors, etc...
Ask each to write a short letter telling your spouse what
they mean to them, what they appreciate about them, &
put them in a scrapbook to give to her.

The Big Date

Take her to a romantic restaurant, someplace with low
lights, expensive food and atmosphere. Arrange to have a
musician (violin or sax) play a couple of numbers; pick a
place with fancy décor and low lighting. Get approval
from the restaurant for music.

During the Date

Spend some time sharing with your spouse what she
means to you, what you appreciate about her, what is
special about her... then give her the scrapbook of the
things others have said about her.

Closing the Night Out

Stop for a dip of gelato or pastries on the way home.

DATE ALA MODE

Pre Date Prep

Buy two bottles of bubbles and some sidewalk chalk.

The Big Date

Drive to friends, family, enemies & strangers homes... sneak in and write silly messages on their sidewalk with the chalk... spend time between houses blowing bubbles at stop signs.

During the Date

After you get tired or too hungry to keep writing, head to a restaurant with home style food and pie... Talk about some of your favorite memories from your school years- K thru college.

Closing the Night Out

If your car seat allows it, ask her to snuggle next to you on the way home... touch her hair or rub your hand on her shoulder... make sure you have mood music playing on the CD player in the car.

I Love U Forever

Pre Date Prep

Make arrangements to take her on a horseback ride; also, have a sharp pocket knife with you to be able to carve your initials on a tree with.

The Big Date

Go horseback riding, and find a tree to carve your initials on. Pick your favorite BBQ place to eat at...

During the Date

Enjoy horseback riding... Later go eat some great BBQ, and be sure and lick the BBQ sauce off of each other's fingers! Talk about what you want your life to look like 5, 10 & 20 years from now.

Closing the Night Out

When you get home, tell her you're not ready for the date to end, and go for a walk around your neighborhood holding hands. Ask her what she has going on tomorrow, next week, and a few months down the road... Listen close, and from what you hear, find a way to do something special for her.

CRUISING WITH THE TOP DOWN

Pre Date Prep

Rent or borrow a convertible for the evening; pack a picnic dinner and make sure your MP# player is loaded up with romantic music.

The Big Date

Flip a coin over which direction to drive, and go for a drive in the country; stop along the way and have a picnic dinner; if it rains, put up the top, and go to a park where you can picnic under a pavilion.

During the Date

Put the radio on her favorite station, or have some of her favorite CD's with you in the car... Also, stop in at a convenience store and pick out matching, goofy or cool sunglasses for the trip.

Closing the Night Out

Both of you talk about your favorite memories of growing up, and about your favorite memories dating, and of your marriage.

GET AWAY GO AWAY

Pre Date Prep

Call & make reservations for dinner or for a cottage at a Bed & Breakfast… Make sure and get a cottage with all the amenities- nice view, hot tub, etc.

The Big Date

The day before the getaway, surprise her by letting her know you'll be kidnapping her for a romantic getaway the next day, and tell her what time she needs to be packed and ready to leave. If she needs any kind of special clothing or other items, let her know that too.

During the Date

Ask her to tell brainstorm a list of places she'd like to go, or things she would like own. Try to talk about anything but work or the kids.

Closing the Night Out

Sit together on the front porch of the cottage, or snuggle under the covers.... or both.

STRIKE A POSE

Pre Date Prep

Sort through old pictures of both of you, & pull out your favorites; buy a small picture album and put them in it for her; write her a short love note in the front of the album.

The Big Date

Have a photographer meet you somewhere and take a photo shoot of the two of you. Make sure that you warned your spouse this was going to happen. After the pictures, head out for a fun dinner.

During the Date

While you're waiting on the food, each of you make a list of famous DEAD people you have liked to meet, and WHY; and a list of LIVING people you'd want to meet, and talk about WHY you would; brainstorm for ways to meet on or two of the people on each of your list.

Closing the Night Out

Give her the album, and look through the pictures together. Plan on putting some of the pictures from this evening into the album.

AQUA-MASSAGE ME

Pre Date Prep

Make reservations for a Water Massage or a regular massage for both of you. Also make reservations for her to have her nails done that evening at her normal nail place... Women typically like having a manicure/pedicure done at the same place they usually use, so if you don't know where that is, ask.

The Big Date

A water massage booth is a unique twist on a massage, but if you don't have one of those as a local option, then schedule a standard massage.

During the Date

After the water massage, go to the Food Court at a local mall and order a little something from each of the food places, and have your own private smorgasbord.

Closing the Night Out

After dinner, take her to someplace in the mall to get her nails done, or take her to "her" place for a manicure/pedicure.

HOME SPA TREATMENT

Pre Date Prep

Do some snooping with her friends, siblings, etc. and find out her favorite aromas; buy candles, body sprays & bath soaps in that aroma from Bath & Body Works, & a dozen roses.

The Big Date

Do a Spa night at home. Make sure there are no kids in the house, and draw a bath for her with her favorite bath soaps... light candles in the bath and bedroom, and spread the rose petals across the sink area, and on the bed. Cook her favorites for dinner while she's enjoying her pampering.

During the Date

Play soft music of her favorite group or artist, and just talk while she relaxes.

Closing the Night Out

Offer to rub her feet, her back, and her neck... whatever she would enjoy. Make sure that you have her favorite cold drink there as well. Ask her to think about what the things are that she loves for you to do for her the most, and how you can help her more around the house.

BIRTHDAY MUSIC TIME

Pre Date Prep

Go to a local music/bookstore, and buy her a gift certificate (enough for at least one CD- but 2 or 3 would be better!) Also, steal her driver's license, or anything else with her birthday on it.

The Big Date

Head to the music/bookstore and listen to music; each pick out a CD to buy; give her the gift certificate for hers. Take her to a restaurant that does silly stuff for people on their birthday for dinner; tell them it's her birthday, and when she tries to deny it with her driver's license, she won't be able to... ask them to give her the birthday treatment.

During the Date

Stay with her; don't wander off in the store. Listen to what she's listening to, and ask her what she likes about them.

Closing the Night Out

Go to a drive in for an ice cream dessert, and talk about your favorites together; music, types of movies, books, TV shows.

CHICK FLICK MOVIE TIME

Pre Date Prep

Make reservations at a fancy hotel. You should check into the room before hand, and have on hand there her favorite flowers, candles burning and lights dimmed.

The Big Date

Take her to a "chick flick" movie, something mushy and romantic... at different times during the movie, kiss her softly on the hand, on the cheek and on the lips... at the end of the movie, when the lights go up, kiss her passionately and long, making people climb over you to get out... Then spend the night at a fancy hotel.

During the Date

Before heading to the hotel, stop at a fancy Italian restaurant to eat dinner... Have her make a list for you of her sizes, favorite colors, scents, flowers, desired gifts for the future.

Closing the Night Out

Don't allow yourself to make this a time that's all about the physical... spend time just talking, snuggling, and enjoying being together.

Leavin' On a Jet Plane

Pre Date Prep

Book your airfare for a roundtrip ticket for that day, or next day if you plan to stay over; secretly pack her bags for her.

The Big Date

Fly to a large metro area within a couple of hundred miles on a cheap fare, do dinner and fly home.

During the Date

Eat either at a restaurant in or near the airport; if you plan to stay over, take her shopping, site seeing or both.

Closing the Night Out

Hold hands on the plane, in the airport, taxi, wherever! Have her pick out a souvenir to help remember the trip.

TAKE IT FOR A TEST DRIVE

Pre Date Prep

Make a list of the dealerships in town with the kinds of cars you would like to test drive- BMW, Lexus, Cadillac, or Corvette- and make an orderly plan for getting from one to the other.

The Big Date

Pick several auto dealerships, and test drive the most expensive cars on the lot.

During the Date

Go to a hibachi Japanese restaurant, and watch them cook your food.... be sure and leave some so that they can make an aluminum foil swan for you to take leftovers home in.

Closing the Night Out

Stop and buy a new key ring for her, or something to hang off of her key ring to remember the night.

THRIFTY NIGHT OUT

Pre Date Prep

Look up the addresses of at least 3 or 4 thrift stores, and swing by and check them out beforehand if you can... Make plans on the order in which you want to go to them.

The Big Date

Go to three thrift stores, and give each other a $5 budget apiece at each one... find something special, something practical and something wacky for each other.

During the Date

Try on and try out as many fun or silly things as you can at each store... see if you can take turns coming up with imaginary stories about the people to whom weird, unusual or special items you find used to belong to.

Closing the Night Out

Go to fun pizza joint, and each order your favorite half of a pizza... just have fun... And make a list of at least 5 things of EACH OTHER'S that you would want to give away to the Thrift Store.

PRIME CUT

Pre Date Prep

If you live near a lake, find a nice restaurant with a view of the lake. Be sure and request a table with a view of the lake; also, borrow a pickup, load up a bunch of pillows and blankets for stargazing after dinner; finally, buy her favorite kind of cookies.

The Big Date

After they give you your menus and before the waiter comes to take your order, ask her what she would like to eat; then order for her... be sure to include appetizers, but not dessert.

During the Date

During the dinner, spend a lot of time holding hands and looking into her eyes while you talk; tell her the things you remember most about her when you first met her, your first date, first kiss, first whatever.

Closing the Night Out

Go find some place down by the lake that is close enough to hear the water, but clear enough to see the sky... lay out the pillows and blanket (it can get cold down near the water at night), and just spend time listening to the radio and talking.

PUT IT IN REVERSE

Pre Date Prep

Buy his and her T-shirts with a funny sayings to wear on your date.

The Big Date

Make it a reverse date... Go to a frozen yogurt or ice cream place for a custom dessert first, then head to an Indian or Thai restaurant for a little bit of spice in your evening.

During the Date

Brainstorm for unusual, creative or fun things you could do on your next three dates.

Closing the Night Out

Stop by a drug store and each of you buy a romantic card for the other... give them to each other at bed time.

Workin' at the Car Wash

Pre Date Prep

Buy some shoe polish (get the kind that is especially designed for writing on car windows).

The Big Date

Write cute or funny messages on the car windows of your friends or the church staff.

During the Date

Go wash your car together, using the robotic car wash… Spend the time in the car wash kissing… Rinse, lather and repeat as many times as desired.

Closing the Night Out

Eat dinner at a drive-in… and no onions allowed! Share with each other 5 things you would like to do before you die, and why.

Hoop It Up

Pre Date Prep

Buy a cute necklace, chain or ring to give as a present that evening.

The Big Date

Attend a sporting event. Buy foam fingers or noise makers to cheer with, and eat hot dogs at the game.

During the Date

Sneak up to a vendor- preferably popcorn- and ask him if you can hid your gift in a box, and then have him come quickly to your seat and sell it to you. Don't forget to tip him for helping out!

Closing the Night Out

See if you can get your fingers signed by some of the athletes, then go out for a smoothie.

JAZZ IT UP

Pre Date Prep

Buy her a rainbow assortment of carnations; tell her she is the treasure at the end of the rainbow.

The Big Date

Eat dinner at a place with lots of different appetizers; each of you order a couple of appetizers as your meal, and then share. Try a dessert you've never had to top it all off.

During the Date

After dinner, go listen to the live jazz music in the parking lot of 61st & Yale.

Closing the Night Out

Talk about your favorite high school memories, whether they were together or separate.

FANCY SCHMANCY

Pre Date Prep

Buy her favorite candy bar or candy, and give it to her as you start out on the date.

The Big Date

Eat a romantic dinner at someplace expensive. Try the duck, surf and turf or something that's unique to that restaurant.

During the Date

Read to each other from the book "Sheet Music" by Dr. Kevin Lehman, or from the Song of Solomon in the Bible.

Closing the Night Out

Finish the night at an upscale coffee shop, and talk about your sex life; what you like, don't like, and what could make it even better.

PICNIC IN THE PARK

Pre Date Prep

Trade babysitting favors with friends who have children so that she doesn't have to worry about getting childcare for the kids.

The Big Date

Stop off at KFC or other fried chicken place, and get chicken dinner for two "to go"; then take her to a picnic to park. If there's a location near a fountain or water for your picnic, that's a bonus.

During the Date

Lay a blanket on the ground, and relax and eat… Talk about what your dreams are for your kids, and for each other in the future… Take a Frisbee, and play Frisbee together.

Closing the Night Out

Stop at a convenience store on the way home, and be creative as you make yourselves flavored drinks for the ride home.

A Shot in the Dark

Pre Date Prep

Buy 2 disposable cameras, one for each of you…Go to the local zoo, and take pictures of each other with the animals… look for unusual or funny shots to take.

The Big Date

Go to a restaurant that NEITHER of you have ever eaten at before (YOU pick it BEFORE the date begins), and order something you've never eaten before.

During the Date

Talk about food- what you'd like to try sometime, what is gross, what you love.

Closing the Night Out

Order two desserts… spend time sharing your dessert; if you're feeling very romantic, feed each other dessert.

BACK TO NATURE

Pre Date Prep

Gather up camping gear, or make reservations at a cabin at one of the state lodges; pack for her if you are able.

The Big Date

Get away for the evening and the next day for a night and day back to nature… Take food to cook at the cabin, or make reservations ahead of time to eat someplace local, and outdoorsy.

During the Date

Go for a walk, take an evening swim in the lake or river if it's warm enough, and just relax.

Closing the Night Out

Make a list for each other of what you like most about your spouse; things they do, choices they've made, the way they look, what others think about them, etc.; then share your lists with each other.

GIRL'S IN CHARGE

NINE RULES FOR THE NIGHT

(and every night for that matter!)

1) He still needs to open every door for you!!!

2) Listen a lot, and remember he's the most important person in your life!!!

3) Do everything you can to make this a night he'll remember forever!!!

4) Try to stick to the guidelines for your date as close as you can; unless you can do better; you may mix & match items from the list if you choose!!!

5) Fix your hair, perfume up, do everything you can to look awesome for the date!!!

6) Wear something nice, and try to look sharp for him– it's a date!

7) If you need childcare for your kids, then you arrange for it, and confirm it the day before!!!

8) If you run into someone you know while on the date, politely & quickly GET AWAY!!!

9) Touch, talk, smile, laugh, kiss, hug... a bunch!!!

SHIRTS & TACOS

Pre Date Prep

Buy him a box of candy… make sure at least one of them has nuts in it… attach a note that says "Life is like a box of chocolates… Every now and then there's one that's nuts… and I'm nuts about YOU!"

The Big Date

Go to the mall, and shop for and each buy a funny t-shirt for the other, with a funny picture or saying on it that you think fits your spouse! Then head to a Mexican restaurant, and take turns sharing food.

During the Date

Spend some time in silence, gazing into each other's eyes; then spend some time talking about places you each want to visit on vacation- make plans if you want!

Closing the Night Out

Turn the shower on and let it run until it's hot, and have him take a shower… but you not alone!

GOODWILL EACH OTHER

Pre Date Prep

Write a "Thank You" note to his parents for all he has meant to you; make a copy to give to him on the date, and mail the original to his parents before the date.

The Big Date

Go to the a Flea Market or a thrift store... give each other a budget-$10 to buy something wacky for yourself, and $10 to buy something totally awesome for your mate.

During the Date

Go to a nice steakhouse for inner... find one that's kind of fancy... While you're waiting on dinner, each of you make a list of 5 things you like about your spouse, and share those with each other.

Closing the Night Out

Sit in the car in the driveway and cuddle for 15 minutes.

BOWLING FOR YOUR BABY

Pre Date Prep

Check with a local shirt printer or monogram shop and have a bowling shirt for him printed that says, "World's Greatest Husband!"

The Big Date

Take him bowling; order a full supply of hot dogs, nachos and soda to eat while you bowl. See who can bowl the best game, and then try bowling the 2nd game using the opposite arm!

During the Date

Take turns sharing your most favorite memories of time with each other.

Closing the Night Out

Change the sheets on your bed at home, as well as the pillow covers; light some candles to set the mood and spend time snuggling and listening to his favorite music.

PICNIC IN THE GARDEN

Pre Date Prep

Buy him one daisy, with the note attached– "He loves me, he loves me not"; make sure there are an odd number of petals on the daisy!

The Big Date

Rush home, change into shorts and a t-shirt, stop by a fast food restaurant, and have a picnic lunch at your favorite local park or botanical garden.

During the Date

Talk about what you would like to own, people you'd like to meet or experiences you'd like to have.

Closing the Night Out

Write "I Love You" on the bathroom mirror with soap after he goes to sleep.

MAKE OUT MOVIE

Pre Date Prep

Ask your husband's best friend to help you buy a present that he's certain your husband would like- give him a budget.

The Big Date

Go to the dollar movie, then take him to a classy sidewalk café for a fun dinner. Try a unique appetizer to kick off the dinner.

During the Date

Kiss a lot during the movie; take turns initiating the kiss; be sure and tell him that you're taking turns, or he won't get it.

Closing the Night Out

Bring him chocolate covered strawberries, or strawberries and powdered sugar, as you get ready for bed.

Rib Tickler Cowboy

Pre Date Prep

Buy a nice inexpensive bracelet, neck chain or ball cap, whichever you think he'd like the most.

The Big Date

Go horseback riding; give him his gift, then head out to any great rib or BBQ joint. Order a platter with a variety of meats and share it. Leave room for a big, decadent dessert!

During the Date

Talk about the most fun you've ever had with your clothes on; and the most fun you've had with your clothes off.

Closing the Night Out

Have a bouquet of "I Love You" balloons waiting for him when you get back.

PICK A PIC & BOOK A BOOK

Pre Date Prep

Buy a small bottle of his favorite cologne or aftershave (get advice from one of his close friends if you don't know).

The Big Date

Check out a local bookstore/coffee shop, and with a $15 limit, find the funniest, wackiest book that you think your spouse would like; if you don't have a bookstore, then check out the book selection at Sam's Club or Wal-Mart. Spend time looking over your book selections over dinner.

During the Date

Take your wedding pictures with you, and over dinner at sandwich shop or burrito hut. Spend time looking back through your pictures; talk about some of your fond memories of that day, especially ones you have about him.

Closing the Night Out

Stop and order one banana split, two spoons. Give him the cologne/aftershave there, and put a dab of it on him.

A Shady Kind of Date

Pre Date Prep

Buy him a new pair of sunglasses... also, get a basket, and preorder your picnic lunch of sandwiches, chips, cookies & drinks at Subway or a family owned sandwich shop. Pick it all up right before the date.

The Big Date

Drive to a nearby lake, give him his new shades, and spend time walking barefoot along the shoreline, or dangling them off of a dock.

During the Date

As you eat your picnic lunch, each one spend 10 minutes writing a love note to your spouse.

Closing the Night Out

Go to Sonic or another drive-in restaurant, and order one large drink, and two straws.

SMELLS LIKE TEEN SPIRIT

Pre Date Prep

Purchase his favorite aftershave or cologne and give it to him that evening.

The Big Date

Go to an amusement park or family fun center. Ride the rides, and try not to throw up! Follow up your crazy fun with dinner at the park, or swing over to a local buffet and eat as much as your stomach can handle!

During the Date

Talk about the "firsts" in your life; first time you rode a roller coaster, first time you met, first date, first kiss, first Christmas, first time you said I love you, etc.

Closing the Night Out

Stop at a Java Dave's or Starbucks and enjoy some overpriced coffee.

FLIRT THE NIGHT AWAY

Pre Date Prep

Purchase a cheap watch, and have it inscribed on the back with something like "I always have time for you".

The Big Date

Go shopping, and buy matching ball caps, shirts, SOMETHING... after shopping, then go to Joe's Crab Shack or Hard Rock Café for a fun dinner... and be sure and tell them it's his birthday... You might want to buy matching shirts there to remind you of the date.

During the Date

Flirt with each other during the date; lead the way in doing this, and he'll catch on... During the date, talk about what each of you remember as your favorite birthday memories.

Closing the Night Out

Have a package of his favorite ice cream waiting at home, and make him a bowl with all his favorite toppings.

DEDICATED TO THE ONE YOU LOVE

Pre Date Prep

Buy a romantic mushy card, and actually write your own note on it too– something longer than "Love, (your name).

The Big Date

Play miniature golf; then take him to an artisan pizza or authentic Italian restaurant for dinner.

During the Date

Call several radio stations and ask them to play and dedicate your favorite songs to each other.

Closing the Night Out

Stop on the front porch before you enter your house and kiss him passionately, look into his eyes and tell him what it is about him that makes him so attractive to you.

THE SUN WILL COME OUT TOMORROW

Pre Date Prep

Buy him a CD from his favorite artist, or one that he has been wanting, and give it to him.

The Big Date

Take him to a musical or local Broadway production, and make sure you get all dressed up!

During the Date

Hold hands during the program, and look into each other's eyes during the romantic songs.

Closing the Night Out

After the show, split a large fries and coke at Burger King, and talk about what your dreams are for 10 & 20 years from now.

MALL EXPEDITION

Pre Date Prep

Count the number of days that you have been together, and have a cookie decorated at the mall and waiting, saying "Happy (# of) days!"

The Big Date

Go on a Mall Treasure Hunt at your favorite mall; take $10 each, and 30 minutes, and buy as many fun or cute trinkets for each other.

During the Date

Meet back at the food court, and feed each other whatever food you order; talk about the most unique people you've ever met, the most unusual presents you've ever received, the most peculiar place you've ever been–all of the weird things.

Closing the Night Out

Spend 10 minutes of time brainstorming for your next date; find a date on the calendar and book it.

TEDDY CONSTRUCTION

Pre Date Prep

Buy him a T-shirt that will fuel his ego... something like "World's Greatest Dad", "World's Greatest Husband", "World's Greatest Lover", whatever you think would stroke his ego.

The Big Date

Go to burrito shack and have them build you each a custom burrito for dinner.   Afterwards, take him to the "Build a Teddy Bear" Store, and let him build his own personalized teddy bear

During the Date

Kiss at every stoplight, or every time you pass a red car.

Closing the Night Out

Find a restaurant known for their desserts, and share a piece of pie to finish the evening. Give him his shirt, & talk about what you each would like for your next birthday or Christmas.

ON THE WATERFRONT

Pre Date Prep

Brainstorm for a wild, not so expensive gift... the best way to do that is to thumb through the Yellow Pages- give yourself a spending limit of $20, and see what you can come up with.

The Big Date

Walk along a river or water walkway, and take a basket with food & drinks to snack on; sandwiches or chicken drumsticks are perfect for a picnic... spaghetti is not.

During the Date

Watch the sunset together, and kiss as the sun is setting... When you get back to the car, give him his gift.

Closing the Night Out

Swing by a custard shop or Cold Stone Creamery to get dessert... talk about what makes you really– really happy, sad, scared, excited, angry, aroused.

SOUNDTRACK OF YOUR LIFE

Pre Date Prep

Buy him a DVD or movie Video that is his favorite; it should be one that you know he really enjoyed seeing, or that he really wishes he had seen when it came out, but he didn't... If you'd rather, a gift certificate to a video rental store could substitute here.

The Big Date

Check around Tulsa for any concerts that are going on that evening that you think he might like and make plans to attend.

During the Date

Follow it up with dinner at his favorite kind of restaurant- if you don't know his favorite kind of food, ask him!

Closing the Night Out

Sit and talk about what you think are the most attractive traits of your spouse, both internal & external. If the weather is good, sit under the stars someplace private and snuggle; if not, go to IHOP and do the same thing; when you get home, see if he wants to watch his movie together.

MY MOST FAVORITE THING

Pre Date Prep

Take out an ad in your local newspaper, declaring your love for your spouse, and give a copy of it to him on the date; or make a sign and post it at a prominent exit off of the highway.

The Big Date

Attend a local sports game or event... eat hot dogs at the game, or when it's through, head to Wendy's for a late night dinner... but make it a little fancy– bring along a cloth tablecloth, and a candle to make it romantic.

During the Date

Buy trinkets- pennants, caps, foam fingers, etc. for each other.

Closing the Night Out

Make a list of your sizes, favorite colors, favorite scents, aftershave/perfume, foods, stores to shop in, restaurant, and any other favorites- swap lists and surprise each other with the next week.

LET'S MONKEY AROUND

Pre Date Prep

Buy him a stuffed monkey, and attach the note "Let's monkey around".

The Big Date

Play Laser tag together; after playing some high tech "Hatfield's & McCoy's", shooting unsuspecting children with laser pistols, go pig out on some hillbilly BBQ.

During the Date

While playing laser tag, work as a team to gang up and take out everyone else, starting with the small, weak and helpless people playing.

Closing the Night Out

Go get a banana split & give him his monkey! While you're there, talk about what you each think the BEST EVER things are… the best movies, music, song, actor/actress, or any other top of the charts.

Fun a la Mode

Pre Date Prep

Buy 1 or 2 one-time use cameras, as well as buying or finding matching shirts to wear on your date.

The Big Date

Go to a local go-kart track or family fun center. Ride the go-karts, play the games, act goofy, and after you've played, go to dinner, but make sure it's a place that has great desserts.

During the Date

Take a one-time use camera, and have as many different people as you can find to take pictures of the two of you.

Closing the Night Out

At the restaurant order 2 different pieces and kinds of dessert each, and share; switch when you've eaten half of each of yours.

Putting Down Some Roots

Pre Date Prep

Buy a matching pair of goofy shirts for the two of you, and wear them on the date.

The Big Date

Go to a nursery, Lowes or someplace similar and spend time shopping for special plants, bushes or trees; buy one that you can call "your" tree or bush, and plant it together the next day.

During the Date

Talk about what the most important things are to each of you for building a strong relationship, a strong family, a strong faith.

Closing the Night Out

Go to a hamburger or sub sandwich restaurant, and build each other's dinner... and then take turns feeding each other your sandwich and sides.

GLORY DAYS

Pre Date Prep

Put together a small ice chest complete with his favorite pop, candies and snacks.

The Big Date

Go to the drive in movie... if it's a good movie, watch the movie a little; if it's not, then find something else to do... since the movie starts late, you'll want to eat dinner before the movie... try a small locally owned pizza joint with atmosphere.

During the Date

Take some breaks from the car and walk around the drive in. Talk about your favorite experiences in high school. If you have pictures of your high school days, bring them to dinner for a fun trip down memory lane.

Closing the Night Out

Before bed, offer to give him a back rub or foot rub.

I STILL DO

Pre Date Prep

Check in the paper for a wedding taking place at one of the large churches in your city or metro area, and find directions; also, buy an inexpensive sports watch for him. Also, pack two pocket spiral pads and something to write with.

The Big Date

Rush home, dress up nice, and invite yourself to complete strangers wedding... stay for cake and punch; after the wedding & reception, take him to eat at a lodge or outdoors themed restaurant. Be sure to call for reservations.

During the Date

During the ceremony write love notes back and forth to each other on the spiral pads.

Closing the Night Out

Stop at McDonalds on the way home for a sundae; come up with as many fun ways to celebrate your next five or ten wedding anniversaries.

MY KIND OF COUPONS

Pre Date Prep

If you have one, great; if not, then borrow an old Polaroid camera, and buy at least a 20 shot package of film. Also, make him a coupon book with coupons redeemable buy you, for whatever- a back rub, a boy's night out, a romantic evening, whatever you can come up with; try to come up with at least 10 coupons of things he would like.

The Big Date

Take a Polaroid camera and have strangers take pictures of you both (waving, kissing, acting silly, striking a pose) along a waterfront, at the mall, the grocery store, WHEREVER & WHATEVER! Find a fun restaurant.

During the Date

Over your favorite soda, each of you finish the following statements- Love is, Sadness is, Happiness is, Anger is, Peace is, etc... Then give him the Coupon book you've made for him.

Closing the Night Out

Take a walk in the moonlight... hold hands and stop & kiss every block or every five minutes.

Sleepwear or Not to Wear

Pre Date Prep

Buy him a gift certificate to Victoria's Secret.

The Big Date

Go to Victoria's Secret together, and have him pick out something for you with the gift certificate together... Then go to Dillards, J.C. Penny's or Wal-Mart– somewhere, anywhere and pick out some night wear for him too!

During the Date

Over dinner at his favorite kind of restaurant (Mexican, Chinese, whatever), answer the following question... "If you could have five wishes, what would they be, and why?" Take turns sharing your wishes.

Closing the Night Out

Go home for a while, if there are no kids there, and try on your new sleepwear... If they are home, then find a coffee bar or frozen custard stand to enjoy some time together.

I Don't Wanna Grow Up

Pre Date Prep

Buy him a trophy, and have a name plate put on it calling him "The World's Best Friend".

The Big Date

Go to a kid's pizza and game center, and play games and eat pizza– act like a kid and have some fun   .

During the Date

Over dinner, answer the following questions- 'What do you want to be remembered for?"; "If you had only had one day to live, what would you do during that day?"; "What things can I do today & tomorrow to make you feel special?"

Closing the Night Out

Stop for dessert at an ice cream or frozen yogurt joint. Have them build one big Sundae or Banana Split, with two spoons to share.

ICE, ICE BABY

Pre Date Prep

Even if it's warm outside, dig out a sweatshirt for each of you in case you need it for ice skating... Also, buy him a gift that relates to his favorite sport- a new golf glove, running shorts or shoes, fishing pole.

The Big Date

Take him to a local ice arena or skating rink, and go ice skating.

During the Date

Go to your favorite Sushi or Thai place for dinner, and over dinner talk about what you think the perfect house would be like... the perfect job... the perfect vacation.

Closing the Night Out

Stop at a drive-in on the way home, and order slushies for dessert... or hot chocolate! Give him the gift you purchased while you're there, and let him know that what's important to him is important to you.

SKATING INTO THE GOLDEN YEARS

Pre Date Prep

Buy a decorative candle & use it in a basket you prepare with a cloth tablecloth, nice silverware, crystal glasses & cloth napkins.

The Big Date

Take him roller skating. Take him to his favorite fast food restaurant or to a classic American diner, but set the table nice with tablecloth, napkins, candle, crystal and silverware.

During the Date

Talk about what you want to do when you retire. Discuss your savings and financial investments, and ideas for helping to build your financial nest egg.

Closing the Night Out

Stop for a snow cone for a great after dinner treat.

Vow to Vow Again

Pre Date Prep

If possible, contact the minister who married you, and arrange to have him meet you somewhere romantic to perform a renewal of your vows.

The Big Date

Meet the minister at a prearranged location, and have him do a repeat or a renewal of your wedding vows.

During the Date

Take your wedding pictures with you, and following the wedding, and over a romantic dinner at a snooty Italian restaurant, pull out the pictures.

Closing the Night Out

Talk about what your favorite memories of your wedding day were; funny, serious, sexy– all of them! Before you go to bed that night, tell him WHY if you had it to do all over again, you WOULD marry him all over again.

SCRAPPING OVER DINNER

Pre Date Prep

Make a list of the most important people in his life-parents, best friend, kids, boss, teachers, neighbors, etc... ask each of them to write a short (or long) letter telling your spouse what they mean to them, or what they appreciate about them... put them together in scrapbook to give to him.

The Big Date

Take him to a romantic restaurant, some place with low lights, expensive food and atmosphere. Arrange to have a musician (violinist or saxophonist) to play a couple of numbers at your table.

During the Date

Spend some time sharing with your spouse what he means to you, what you appreciate about him, what is special about him... then give him the scrapbook of the things that others have said about him.

Closing the Night Out

Stop off for a dip of him favorite ice cream on the way home.

Amateur Vandals

Pre Date Prep

Buy two bottles of bubbles and some sidewalk chalk.

The Big Date

Drive to friends, family, enemies & strangers homes... sneak in and write silly messages on their sidewalk with the chalk... spend time between houses blowing bubbles at stop signs.

During the Date

After you get tired or too hungry to keep writing, head out to a unique German, Thai or other ethnic restaurant for dinner... Talk about some of your favorite memories from your school years- K thru college.

Closing the Night Out

If your car seat allows it, snuggle next to him on the way home... touch his hair or rub your hand on his shoulder... make sure you have mood music playing on the stereo in the car.

Giddy Up

Pre Date Prep

Make arrangements to take him on a horseback ride; also, have a sharp pocket knife with you, and ask him to carve both of your initials on a tree with it– it'll make him feel macho.

The Big Date

Go horseback riding, and find a tree to carve your initials on.

During the Date

If you can, stop and have a picnic while you're out riding... If not, then pick your favorite BBQ place, and go eat... Be sure and lick the BBQ sauce off of each other's fingers! Talk about what you want your life to look like 5, 10 & 20 years from now.

Closing the Night Out

When you get home, tell him you're not ready for the date to end, and if you can (no kids, please), go for a walk around your neighborhood holding hands. Ask what he has going on tomorrow, next week, next month... Listen close, and from what you hear, find something special to do for him.

DRIVING ME CRAZY

Pre Date Prep

Rent or borrow a convertible for the evening; pack a picnic dinner and a portable MP3 player with a romantic music (Kenny G, or go to Wal-Mart and buy something that says "love songs" on it.

The Big Date

Flip a coin over which direction to drive, and go for a drive in the country; stop along the way and have a picnic dinner; if it rains, put up the top, and go to a park where you can picnic under a pavilion.

During the Date

Put the radio on his favorite station, or have some of his favorite music with you in the car... Also, stop in at a convenience store or Wal-Mart and pick out matching, goofy or cool sunglasses for the trip.

Closing the Night Out

Both of you talk about your favorite memories of growing up, and about your favorite memories dating, and of your marriage.

B & B FOR YOU AND HE

Pre Date Prep

Call & make reservations for dinner or for a cottage at a Bed & Breakfast. Try and find someplace that you can have some privacy, take quiet walks through nature and just relax.

The Big Date

Get away with him for a few days or a special weekend to a Bed & Breakfast.

During the Date

Try to talk about anything but work or the kids... Ask him to brainstorm a list of places he'd like to go, or things he would like own.

Closing the Night Out

Sit together on the front porch of the cottage or your house you're staying in, or snuggle under the covers.... or do both!

LIVE SHOTS, DEAD SHOTS

Pre Date Prep

Sort through old pictures of the two of you, and pull out your favorites; buy a small picture album and put them in it for him; write him a short love note in the front of the album. Use your phones to have others take pictures of your throughout the night.

The Big Date

Take pictures of the two of you together by a photographer, and order a package of pictures; then go eat dinner at your favorite steakhouse.

During the Date

While you're waiting on the food, each of you make a list of famous DEAD people you have liked to meet, and WHY; and a list of LIVING people you'd want to meet, and talk about WHY you would; brainstorm for ways to meet on or two of the people on each of your list.

Closing the Night Out

Give him the album, and look through the pictures together. Plan on putting some of the pictures from this evening into the album.

SECRET MASSAGE

Pre Date Prep

Call ahead and make reservations at a Water Massage booth or at a local spa; do the same for the nail salon about an appointment there.

The Big Date

Both of you get a "water massage" or real massage, and follow it up with a mani/pedi together.

During the Date

After the massage, go to the Food Court at a local mall and order a little something from each of the food places, and have your own private smorgasbord.

Closing the Night Out

After dinner, take him to someplace in the mall to buy him a shirt or ball cap of his favorite college or pro sports team.

PAMPER YOUR MAN

Pre Date Prep

Buy a dozen roses and take all of the petals off. Play soft music of his favorite group or artist, and just talk while he relaxes.

The Big Date

Do a Spa night at home; make sure there are no kids in the house; for dinner, you prepare his favorite dish, or get something from Chili's to go, come home and put it out on nice dishes.

During the Date

Make sure that you have his favorite cold drink there as well. Draw a bath bubble bath for him... light the candles in the bath and bedroom, and spread the rose petals across the sink area, and on the bed.

Closing the Night Out

Offer to rub his feet, his back, and his neck... whatever he would enjoy. Ask him what the things are that he loves for you to do for him the most, and how you can help him more with day to day pressures and stuff in his life.

SING, SING A SONG

Pre Date Prep

Go to a music store & buy him a gift certificate (enough for at least one CD, or several songs for his MP3 player!) Also, steal his driver's license, or anything else with his birthday on it.

The Big Date

Go to the music store and relax spending time listening to music; each pick out a CD to buy; give him the gift certificate for his; stay with him in in the store; listen to what he's listening to, and ask him what he likes about them.

During the Date

Take him to a fun, loud restaurant for dinner; tell them it's his birthday, and when he tries to deny it with his driver's license, he won't be able to... ask them to give him the birthday treatment.

Closing the Night Out

Go to a drive in for an ice cream dessert, and talk about your favorites together; music, types of movies, books, TV shows.

A Night on the Town

Pre Date Prep

Make reservations at a fancy hotel; you should check into the room before hand, and have on hand there his favorite candy, candles burning and lights dimmed.

The Big Date

Take him to a his favorite kind of movie– action, sci-fi, whatever... at different times during the movie, kiss him softly on the hand, on the cheek and on the lips... at the end of the movie, when the lights go up, kiss him long & passionately, making people climb over you to get out.

During the Date

Then spend the night at a fancy hotel. Before heading to the hotel, stop at your favorite Italian place for some pasta! Have him make a list for you of his sizes, favorite colors, scents, flowers, desired gifts for the future.

Closing the Night Out

Don't allow yourself to make this a time that's all about the physical... spend time just talking, snuggling, enjoying being together.

FLY AWAY

Pre Date Prep

Book your airfare for a roundtrip ticket for that day, or next day if you plan to stay over; secretly pack his bags for him.

The Big Date

Fly to a nearby metro area, preferably someplace that the flight isn't longer than 1 hour. You should be able to book a cheap fare, do dinner and fly home in one day if you want to.

During the Date

Eat either at a restaurant in or near the airport; if you plan to stay over, take him shopping, and to a restaurant that town is known for. Hold hands on the plane, in the airport, taxi, wherever!

Closing the Night Out

Have him pick out a souvenir to help remember the trip.

KING OF THE ROAD

Pre Date Prep

Make a list of the dealerships in town with the kinds of cars you would like to test drive- BMW, Lexus, Cadillac, Corvette- and make an orderly plan for getting from one to the other.

The Big Date

Pick several auto dealerships, and test drive the most expensive cars on the lot.

During the Date

Go to a Hibachi restaurant, and watch them cook your food.... be sure and leave some so that they can make an aluminum foil swan for you to take leftovers home in.

Closing the Night Out

Stop and buy a new key ring for him, or something to hang off of him key ring to remember the night.

THRIFTINESS IS NEXT GOODWILL

Pre Date Prep

Look up the addresses of at least 3 or 4 thrift stores, and swing by and check them out beforehand if you can... Make plans on the order in which you want to go to them.

The Big Date

Go to three thrift stores, and give each other a $5 budget apiece at each one... find something special, something practical and something wacky for each other.

During the Date

Try on and try out as many fun or silly things as you can at each store... see if you can take turns coming up with imaginary stories about the people to whom weird, unusual or special items you find used to belong to.

Closing the Night Out

Go to the best pizza joint, and each order your favorite half of a pizza... just have fun... And make a list of at least 5 things of EACH OTHER'S that you would want to give away to the Thrift Store.

DINNER ON THE LAKE

Pre Date Prep

Call & make reservations at a lakeside restaurant. Be sure and request a table with a view of the lake; also, borrow a pickup, load up a bunch of pillows and blankets for stargazing after dinner; finally, buy his favorite kind of cookies.

The Big Date

Drive to the restaurant on the lake. After they give you your menus and before the waiter comes to take your order, ask him what he would like to eat; then order for him... be sure to include appetizers.

During the Date

During the dinner, spend a lot of time holding hands and looking into him eyes while you talk; tell him the things you remember most about him when you first met him, first date, first kiss, first whatever.

Closing the Night Out

Go find some place down by the lake that is close enough to hear the water, but clear enough to see the sky... lay out the pillows and blanket (it can get cold down near the water at night), and just spend time listening to the radio and talking.

REVERSE DATE

Pre Date Prep

Buy his and her T-shirts with a funny sayings to wear on your date.

The Big Date

Make it a reverse date… Go to get ice cream for dessert first, then head to the strangest restaurant you can find for your main course. End up at a hot night spot, and top off the night with an appetizer.

During the Date

Brainstorm for unusual, creative or fun things you could do on your next three dates.

Closing the Night Out

Stop by someplace that sells greeting cards, and search until you find the perfect card for each other. Then you can buy a romantic card for the other… give them to each other at bed time after you've had a chance to write a romantic or sexy note to each other on the card.

SHOE POLISH SHOWS YOU CARE

Pre Date Prep

Buy some shoe polish (get the kind that is especially designed for writing on car windows).

The Big Date

Write cute or funny messages on the car windows of your friends or the church staff.

During the Date

Go wash your car together, using the robotic car wash… Spend the time in the car wash kissing… Rinse, lather and repeat as many times as desired.

Closing the Night Out

Eat dinner at your local drive in or hamburger joint, and no onions allowed. Share with each other 5 things you would like to do before you die, and why.

BATTER, BATTER, BATTER SWING

Pre Date Prep

Buy a cap of his favorite sports team, and give it to him as you head out on the trip. Double his fun with a matching shirt!

The Big Date

Attend a baseball game local baseball game, and try to pick out a night when they are giving away bobble heads, ball caps or some other freebie.

During the Date

Buy foam fingers or noise makers to cheer with, and eat hot dogs at the game. Take your ball gloves so you can try to catch a foul ball!

Closing the Night Out

See if you can get your fingers signed by some of the players, then go out for a smoothie.

TASTE THE RAINBOW

Pre Date Prep

Buy him a big bag of Rainbow Skittles; tell him he is the treasure at the end of the rainbow. Also, scope out someplace in your town that plays live music.

The Big Date

Eat dinner at a nice steakhouse. Order appetizers, and try a dessert you've neither ever had before.

During the Date

After dinner, go listen to the live music and just enjoy hanging out together. Talk about your favorite high school memories, whether they were together or separate. Find out who your favorite or least favorite teachers, subjects and experiences were.

Closing the Night Out

Stop off for some Rainbow Sherbert at a local ice cream place, or buy some at the grocery store, and share a big bowl when you get home.

CALLING DR. LOVE

Pre Date Prep

Buy his favorite candy bar or candy, and give it to him as you start out on the date.

The Big Date

Eat a romantic dinner an upscale restaurant, with fancy table cloths and multiple forks! Make sure you both dress up in your finest duds.

During the Date

Read to each other from the book "Sheet Music" by Dr. Kevin Lehman, or from the Song of Solomon in the Bible.

Closing the Night Out

Finish the night at Starbucks or a local coffee shop, and talk about your sex life; what you like, don't like, and what could make it even better.

PICNIC PLAYGROUND

Pre Date Prep

Trade babysitting favors with friends who have children so that he doesn't have to worry about getting childcare for the kids.

The Big Date

Stop off at KFC, and get chicken dinner for two "to go"; then take him to a picnic near any fountains or water at a park.

During the Date

Lay a blanket on the ground, and relax and eat. Talk about what your dreams are for your kids, and for each other in the future… Take a Frisbee, and play Frisbee together.

Closing the Night Out

Stop at your favorite convenience store on the way home, and be creative as you make yourselves flavored drinks for the ride home.

YOU CRAZY ANIMAL

Pre Date Prep

Buy 2 disposable cameras, one for each of you.

The Big Date

Go to the City Zoo, and take pictures of each other with the animals… look for unusual or funny shots to take.

During the Date

Go to a restaurant that NEITHER of you have ever eaten at before (YOU pick it BEFORE the date begins), and order something you've never eaten before… Talk about food- what you'd like to try sometime, what is gross, what you love, what you hate.

Closing the Night Out

Order two desserts… spend time sharing your dessert; if you're feeling very romantic, feed each other dessert.

Nature Calls

Pre Date Prep

Gather up camping gear, or make reservations at a cabin at one of the state lodges; pack for him if you are able.

The Big Date

Get away for the evening and the next day for a night and day back to nature… Take food to cook at the cabin, or make reservations ahead of time to eat someplace local, and outdoorsy.

During the Date

Go for a walk, take an evening swim in the lake or river if it's warm enough, and just relax.

Closing the Night Out

Make a list for each other of what you like most about your spouse; things they do, choices they've made, the way they look, what others think about them, etc.; then share your lists with each other.

43413169R00092

Made in the USA
Middletown, DE
08 May 2017